The Herbal Guide for Stables

by Katharine Lark Chrisley, NHC, RMT

Dharmahorse Herbal Guide for Stables

By Katharine Lark Chrisley, NHC, RMT

©Dharmahorse 2011

The advice and experiences in this manual are offered purely for informational purposes. We do not make any claims for *cures* for your animals. A health care practitioner should be consulted for diagnosis and treatment of any disease or injury to your animals. A Holistic Veterinarian is our suggestion.
If you use some of the information in this manual for an animal or for yourself, without input from a Veterinarian or a Physician, you are diagnosing and prescribing. This is your constitutional right, but the author, publisher, distributor and agents of this manual assume no responsibility for your actions.
When using any herb, nutrient or supplement for the first time – give in small doses, building up gradually to the full amount after seeing that there are no adverse reactions. Every being is an individual with unique characteristics and metabolisms.
Many animal lovers are caretakers for several different species – take note cat owners – herbs, oils and medications that are perfectly correct for dogs, horses, humans and others can be toxic, even fatal to cats. This also applies for reptiles, ferrets, birds and exotics. Do not take chances. Contact a practitioner before administering any compound that is unfamiliar or in question. The FDA has not approved any of the following statements.

ALFALFA, *Medicago sativa*, is a legume that makes a fine addition to the diets of horses, dogs and humans by adding minerals, vitamins (especially the precursor to Vitamin A - beta carotene) and complex proteins. Because it can be up to 26%(!) protein (but is usually around 14 to 18%), it is not good to use as the only source of food for the herbivores, especially the browsers like horses: The mature equine requires 11% protein in the diet; the growing horse needs 14%. Excess protein (for all species) is processed and excreted by the renal system.

For us, alfalfa tablets and tea have been taken for centuries to nourish arthritic joints (it neutralizes uric acid) and to make the skin and hair healthy. This is supported by the vitamin A and protein content. Alfalfa is high in Calcium even when grown on poor soil. There are 8 digestive enzymes in alfalfa and saponin properties that bind toxins and deposits for elimination. Alfalfa supports the pituitary gland; its minerals strengthen and heal teeth.

Alfalfa is a premiere food for lactation in all species. When fed to horses, wheat bran is a good addition to the diet to add Phosphorus - the equine diet must have a calcium to phosphorus ratio of - 2 to 1 to 1.5 to 1. The high calcium in alfalfa should be balanced with the wheat bran (other types of bran i.e. rice, oat - are not suggested). We suggest feeding ¾ grass hays and ¼ alfalfa when needed.

The canine diet benefits from alfalfa tablets or tea. The herb helps keep joints nourished and is great for chronic digestive troubles like ulcers. Some allergies are allayed by alfalfa and bee pollen supplements. Of course, use the herbalists' safety ways - dose small amounts at first and watch for any reactions. All metabolisms are unique!

Legumes grown for hay to feed horses, cattle, etc. (including clovers) can have blister beetles in them after the second cutting. Grass hays will not, only legumes attract the deadly beetles that swarm and can be killed, then baled with the hay during the cutting/baling processes. Only a dozen large beetles are necessary to poison a horse (colic symptoms/extreme pain) and activated charcoal, kaolin, bicarbonate of soda and later mineral oil are dosed by the Vet or practitioner to hopefully save the horse. The beetle is from 1/2 to an inch long, can be black or iridescent blue/green or green and black striped. It has a long hind end with wings, is thin.

ALMOND, *Amygdalus dulcis,* nut kernels provide healing and nourishing food and oil. For young animals and humans, the nuts are blanched in boiling water to remove the brown "skin" and the internal white "meat" is ground to a nourishing meal that is added to milk and fed in small amounts often. This food is used for bowel health, coughs and lung disorders and to restore strength during illness. Three almonds eaten daily are said to help resist cancer in humans. Of course, keeping the body nourished and vibrant on all levels will be a deterrent to cancers, parasites, infections and the like (opportunistic invaders!) - As does the nourishing of the body enable it to fight a better fight.

Almond oil and Almond butter are supreme emollients for skin health and can be used on all creatures safely. For wounds and sores on horses, apply several times daily. Use the oil for cracked noses on dogs and for sore eyelids on anyone.

You can find pure Almond Oil at a health food store or the herbalists'.

Remember, all beings are individuals and each metabolism is unique. If you have a reaction from an herb or oil; stop using it immediately.

ANISE seed, *Pimpinella anise*, is an herb we use to prevent and in treatment of colic in horses. It is also great for coughs and lung disorders. We add the powdered herb to a bucket feed using a tablespoon once daily as prevention for horses prone to colic. When a horse is starting to look distressed, we feed a quarter cup of the ground seed in a very wet wheat bran mash with an ounce of milk of magnesia.

We feed it similarly for lung disorders, usually with large amounts of Yarrow tea either dosed carefully into the mouth (keep head low to avoid aspiration into the lungs!) or used to soak the mash.

ASPARAGUS, *Asparagus officinalis,* is a nourishing vegetable that is also a healing herb in Phytotherapy (healing with plants). The shoots (called "sprue") contain *Asparagin* which is a unique crystalline medicine that clears and supports the entire renal system of all animals and people.

Horses, cattle and camelids seek out and devour the plants that grow along ditch banks and near waterways. The roots have medicinal properties as well (for bladder and kidneys). To use the root destroys the plant, of course, so we recommend snapping or cutting the shoots for use. To feed as a remedy for equine bladder or kidney wasting, pain, infection or obstruction - give large animals one handful of raw shoots twice a day for 10 days.

Dogs love steamed Asparagus. You can mash it well after cooking and feed mixed into the ration or on its own to support the system. I give a large dog 1/4 cup twice a day / medium dog one tablespoon twice daily / a small dog one teaspoon twice a day; for 10 days. My dogs actually like their asparagus raw and fed without cooking, it retains the healing enzymes.

When there were recalls of tainted dog foods and many canines were dying from renal failure (caused by the toxins) - I put out the asparagus information through several sites and heard many dogs recovered that perhaps could have died without the asparagus detox.

People will find this delicious healer effective cooked or raw and it makes a great addition to meals 2 or 3 times a week just for nourishment. In times of renal distress - bladder infections, kidney stones, weak urination, burning or pain with urination, etc. - the shoots should be eaten 2 to 3 times daily for 10 days. For children use 4 shoots per dose, for adults use 6 to 10 depending upon weight. This will support and cleanse the system to aid healing.

You can use canned or frozen shoots. Try to use low salt canned asparagus. I keep a few cans handy just in case (also cranberry sauce - another profound renal cleanser and detoxifier of the entire body), while fresh is best - if I need it quickly, the market could be out!

Asparagus also supports joints and aids healing of all infections by relieving the endocrine system, allowing the flow of lymph through the lymphatic system that is a part of all bodies' filtering mechanisms: Liver/Kidneys/Glands - Asparagus is effective support in the healing of jaundice.

BARLEY, *Hordeum vugare*, is a Cereal that is used wild or cultivated. The seed/grain is removed from the whiskered awns for use as food and medicine. The grass leaves are dried and used as straw after harvesting the grain. The barley grain must be rolled (flattened/crimped) before being fed to horses as the small kernels are too hard and would likely just be swallowed or cause choke. Barley flour makes nutritious bread but would form a paste if fed to animals that would choke them.

Pearled Barley is de-husked, polished and dried grain that is a nourishing addition to soups and stews for people. Barley grain is too rich to feed in large amounts to horses, but is a very good addition, in small amounts, to older equines' rations and those with any type of renal disorder.

Barley Water is the most healing form, being used to moisten mashes, dry dog food, as a drink for people and animals or a drench for horses. It is a healer of the kidneys and bladder. To make barley water: crush 2 cups of whole barley grains inside of a cloth bag using a hammer, place into a non-metal container, add 4 cups of water just off the boil and cover to sit for 6 hours, then add 4 cups of tepid water with the juice of a fresh lemon and 4 ounces of raw honey. Mix well and strain the liquid for use. You can adjust the amount to make smaller batches (or larger ones).

BASIL, *Ocimum basilicum*, leaf is sometimes fed for diarrhea and can be chewed to apply to insect bites. Mostly, we use the essential oil of Basil to enhance concentration. *Essential oils* should be diluted in a *carrier oil* (olive or grapeseed). We place 10 drops of Basil oil into 40 drops of carrier oil and rub it into the horse's chest before work, taking the opportunity to smell the aroma on our hands to aid our own concentration.

BEETS, *Beta vulgaris*, are used to increase the body's resistance to disease and to "anti-dote" toxins as well as support clearing of the liver (nature's filter). We can drink the liquid from a can of plain beets as a quick "fix" or dose it to our horse orally as soon as we know of exposure to a toxin. Of COURSE, call a poison control center for emergencies! But when you accidentally spill a mild contaminant on your hands (like gasoline at the pump, simple things that happen, but add up when we absorb them over time) or have to use strong remedies for thrush in a hoof or your dog walks over the just waxed floor - eating red beets or drinking the juice (or both) can help the liver clear the toxic properties that pass through the skin!

I feed horses raw, red beets, chopped up and added (2 big roots per horse) to a mash once daily for 3 to 7 days. Cooked roots and greens (steamed is best) are excellent additions to our own diets and can be fed to dogs (one to four large spoons full according to weight) once a week.

White beets are used to aid the liver when assaulted by alcohol/drug abuse. Sugarbeet pulp is a highly digestible food for horses that provides needed roughage for malnourished, elderly or ill equines. ALWAYS soak beet pulp in cold water for several hours before feeding and add a vitamin / mineral supplement, source of protein (alfalfa or flaxseed meal) and source of fat (safflower oil, flaxseed or even olive oil – remember that corn oil can be inflammatory, so is not a good choice...).

Beetroot is used in Europe to treat cancers. Beets enhance the immune system, nourish tissues and restore the liver. Red beets are used to add red color in a safe, natural way to dog biscuits, cookies, etc. Feeding beets can darken the stool.

BLADDERWRACK is a sea vegetable we use for arthritis; joint soaks, made into a strong infusion (tea) and used as a fomentation. It is fed to horses to strengthen bones, support renal and lung health and to help heal wounds from within. Its high mineral content is what makes it so effective.

BURDOCK *Arctium lappa* - Burdock root is a blood purifier, system cleanser that is considered safe for our dogs, our horses and for us. It is used as a liver tonic, for arthritis, to heal the skin internally and externally and to support glandular/lymphatic health. The root is used and is made into a "decoction" by simmering slowly in water in a *non-metal* pot for a half hour, covered. Or, you can feed the cut and sifted root to horses in their concentrates, one tablespoon every day for 10 to 14 days as a loading dose, one teaspoon per day as maintenance for 28 days. You can give medium size dogs a big pinch of the powder or a capsule daily for 10 days. People take one capsule twice daily for 2 to 4 weeks.

Burdock is one of the roots that animals dig up and eat in the Spring, knowing instinctively that their bodies will benefit from the tonic effect. If you have skin problems, puffiness around glands, have had exposure to pesticides (asparagus should included in this case!) or have been eating poorly, BURDOCK will clean up the systems.

CALENDULA, *Calendula officinalis*, blossoms are fed to horses to support skin health and healing. I've fed it to mare and used homeopathic calendulated oil topically to heal her severe rainrot. It is high in vitamin C, vitamin A and phosphorus. Calendula ointment made with blossoms infused into olive oil and stabilized with bees wax is used to dress wounds, burns, rashes and chapping.

We have used calendula tincture on bruises and strains. It has some good anti-inflammatory properties used externally as well as fed in the bucket feed. I give one or two big handfuls of the dry blossoms daily. It is a good treatment for mud fever / scratches, rainrot, rope burns, eczema and contusions.

CHAMOMILE is "Roman" (*Chamaemelum Nobile*) or "German" (*Matricaria Recutita*). If you have ragweed allergies, Chamomile will probably irritate you because it is related. It has feathery leaves and white, daisy-like flowers. It is known as a blood cleanser and pain reliever. It is used as a tea (infusion) or homeopathically for teething children, sore gums and as a poultice to remove splinters, slivers, stickers (it was said to pull out bullets!) and embedded objects. I just tape a soaked (in warm water) Chamomile tea bag over the object before going to bed at night.

It is an important ingredient in our remedy for tumors and is used in hair rinses to heal the scalp. The tea aids indigestion, irritable bowel and anxiety. Essential oil of Chamomile is expensive, bright blue (it contains azulenes) and is used for stress, eczema, even asthma.

Chamomile can cause contact dermatitis in those prone to reactions and skin allergies. Remember, it is a uterine stimulant, so it can bring on menses, so it is contraindicated for pregnancy!

Chamomile Flower Essence is used for one who is irritable and moody.

It is fed to HORSES to calm them: one small handful of blossoms in the feed per day. The tea can be rubbed on the sore gums of DOGS.

CAYENNE, *Capsicum annum*, is not just a spicy addition to foods, it has several unique medicinal properties. As a blood stopping powder it is safe and effective. On any profusely bleeding wound (except near the eyes or on mucus membranes) the powder can be packed to staunch the blood flow and disinfect. Do not wrap over it.

Cayenne powder can be lightly applied inside of socks to keep your feet warm in the winter and is an ingredient in super warming liniments.

It is full of Vitamin C. A tea can be made with a teaspoon of herb in a cup of boiled water or it can be added to soups to clear the sinuses, ward off colds and infections and support the circulatory system. Cayenne helps stimulate digestion and open blood vessels when taken internally.

The use of Cayenne for horses is mostly as an addition to liniment formulas and as a blood stopping agent. For dogs, its uses are limited to emergency styptic application or careful addition internally **only** *upon advice of a health professional*. Humans can usually ingest Cayenne often; use ointments with Cayenne on arthritic joints; liniments and use in socks for warmth and on bleeding wounds.

I have friends who use Cayenne in capsules to prevent diverticulitis, to keep arteries clear and to "cure" colds! It sure seems to work for them.

CHICKWEED, *Stellaria media*, is a creeping herb with tiny white flowers. It is entirely edible for all animals (although it can be too rich for some if eaten fresh and abundantly!). It is considered a cancer-preventing herb and a premier healer of the digestive tract. It is fed to arthritic horses and used to reduce lipoma/fatty tumors.

Chickweed nourishes the Pineal and Pituitary glands, helping them return to normal function when afflicted. It is full of the mineral - organic Iron - which is necessary for all mammals to transport oxygen and maintain youthfulness. Food additives/preservatives deplete iron from the body which causes anemia, lung and circulatory damage, blood sugar imbalances and weakness.

Chickweed is a mild herb used to gradualy return health to tissues and the whole plant can be fed fresh or dried; or a tea can be made from the dried herb. An infused oil can be made by warming the herb into olive oil for use externally on swollen joints, tumors or fatty deposits.

CLEAVERS, *Galium aparine,* are an important herb for owners of gray horses! They possess strong anti tumor properties which used internally and externally. I have fed the dry, cut and sifted herb to my gray, white and Appaloosa horses for decades. And, because I have lived in a valley where copious amounts of chemicals are just *poured* onto the crops - I feed Cleavers to all of our horses about 6 to 8 months of each year. (Also, I feed burdock root, milk thistle and raw, fresh beets!)

I feed a large handful of the herb daily to a horse in need and give one tablespoon daily on the feed preventively. I often include Cleavers in custom herbal blends for horses because it is FULL of minerals that build and repair bone, muscle, skin, hair (all cutaneous structures) and hoof!

I use Cleavers tincture for people and dogs. I always evaporate the alcohol by placing the drops in hot water before giving to animals. A large dog or human would take 30 drops of tincture twice a day as a loading dose for 10 days; then once daily for maintenance. Medium dogs get between 10 and 15 drops; small dogs get 5 drops.

I feed Cleavers to support the healing of any skin disease or disorder. I believe in it for any tumor or cancer, even within the body because it supports the tissue that is trying to normalize.

Externally: The dry Cleavers herb is used with equal amounts of flaxseed meal mixed into a paste with boiling water to create a poultice for tumors. This can be used on horses, dogs and people.

Cinnamon, *Cinnamomun zeylanicum***,** is an evergreen tree whose dried inner bark is used as a culinary herb / spice and as a medicinal herb for people, horses and dogs. During cold weather, we are treated to hot apple juice with cinnamon sticks infusing within the cups; cookies and pies baked with ground cinnamon; the scent by way of cinnamon essential oil added to potpourris and wreaths about the house. The scent itself has immune boosting, antiseptic and anti-nausea properties.

Cinnamomum cassia is an inferior spice that should not be used for dogs.

Proper cinnamon added to dog diets can help regulate blood sugar, relieve nausea and help stop diarrhea. From a pinch for a tiny dog to a teaspoon fed to a very large dog - Cinnamon can be added (ground) to the daily food for 1 week for digestion and up to 9 months to regulate blood sugar (it is adaptogenic, it normalizes either high or low conditions). It can be baked into biscuits as well.

Horses with conditions like Cushing's Syndrome can be helped with the addition of half ground Cinnamon, half ground Fenugreek seeds to the ration - about 2 tablespoons daily. Horses prone to gassiness or flatulent colic can be aided by a half Cinnamon, half Fennel seed mixture fed daily 1 to 2 teaspoons.

People benefit from Cinnamon regularly in the diet to regulate blood sugar, aid digestion, stimulate warmth in the body and energize the system. It is astringent, helping ease loose bowels; is useful to stop vomiting.

COMFREY, *Symphytum officinale,* is a plant that is easily grown and is the premier herb for injuries of all kinds. It is used externally and internally to heal bruises, broken bones, lacerations (cuts), abrasions (rubbed sores), contusions (wounds with bruising also), burns (heat, chemical and friction) and any swelling or inflammation. To use internally, it must be temporary and no longer than 60 days at a time because it can eventually irritate the liver. Infusions are drunk or dosed in small amounts often. Sometimes tinctures or capsules are taken (according to package directions).

Comfrey is used for Humans, Horses and Dogs.

EXTERNALLY:

Comfrey leaves are brewed as an infusion - steep one handful dried leaves (2 fresh) to 2 quarts pure water just off the boil, covered in a non-metal pot. Let steep for 25 minutes and strain well. The infusion of LEAF is mild and used for infants (externally only, always), small and delicate animals or elderly persons. This infusion is applied COLD to acute injuries and WARM to old, chronic injuries. I use a spray bottle for application.

Comfrey Roots are boiled to make a decoction - one handful dried roots (2 fresh) to one quart of pure water in a non-metal pot. Bring to a boil, cover and simmer for 25 minutes. Then let sit, covered for an hour before straining. Squeeze all the moisture from the herb. I also use a sprayer (or sponge) for the decoction. Apply COLD to acute injuries, WARM to old chronic injuries.

Comfrey Oil is made by heating the roots and leaves in safflower oil.
Comfrey Ointment adds beeswax to the infused oil to form a salve.

The root of the Comfrey plant stimulates the growth and healing of bone cells! It contains allantoin to soothe and stimulate skin cell growth. It used to be called "bone knit" and is a profound healer of bone fractures and injuries to the skull or blows to the eye (especially in HOMEOPATHIC form). Do not use Comfrey until a fracture has been set. Do not use Comfrey on a wound that has debris in it. *Comfrey can heal things too quickly.*

Homeopathic Symphytum is made from Comfrey and is the first thing to dose when a severe injury occurs (along with Homeopathic Arnica or Bellis). It is good for excessive pain, injuries to the cartilage and periosteum that covers the bones. Use it for any injury to the eyeball or head. Homeopathic remedies are usually in small pellet form and you dose humans, horses or dogs the amount suggested on the container - it is not the amount that determines the strength of the healing, but how often it is dosed. The little pellets can be added to bland treats, mixed with water and placed in the mouth or put under the tongue.

CORNSILK, *Zea mays,* is an important nourishing herb - not the silk from fresh corn that you buy at the market to eat (it could have chemicals on it or be genetically engineered), but we are talking about herbal cornsilk purchased from a trusted source. The dry cornsilk can be steeped as an infusion for a renal system cleansing tea. It is a great remedy for incontinence in humans, horses and dogs. Cornsilk is available in capsules as well and is often effectively paired with Uva Ursi herb for the bladder/kidneys.

We often add it by the small handful to the horses' bucket feeds in the autumn to support renal health after a long, hot summer.

Cornsilk crushed into a coarse powder and mixed with hot water makes a drawing poultice that is useful for abscesses and infections - due to its purifying properties.

ECHINACEA, *Echinacea Augustifolia / Echinacea purpurea*, is an effective remedy for bacterial and viral infections. It "boosts" the immune system and therefore is contraindicated for any being with auto-immune diseases. The root and leaves are both used. We tend to use the root for treatments; the leaves for prevention. It contains vitamins and minerals (ZINC, iron, manganese, selenium and silicon) and "undiscovered properties" that make it a premier herb for all infections – from tooth/gum infections to lung disorders to hoof abscesses – added to the bucket feed. We feed a handful of the dried leaves daily to a horse for at least 21 days or a heaping tablespoon of root in the feed for at least 14 days.

For dogs, we usually give a 350 to 475 mg. capsule of Echinacea (medium size dog) twice daily for 2 to 3 weeks.

EYEBRIGHT, *Euphrasia officinalis,* is used as an infusion (tea) *orally to strengthen the eyes and heal disorders* in all species. It can be used as a compress for injuries near the eye and will soothe the sinuses and support healing of throat irritations. It is known to reduce allergic reactions. With consistent use orally and as an eye drop (weak infusion with a pinch of sea salt) *it reverses cataracts in some people and animals.* The eye wash is used to heal styes - another good eye wash for styes is a weak decoction of bayberry bark!

The Eyebright herb can be found in capsules that are convenient for people (use recommended dosage) and for dogs (put 1/2 capsule content in food for small dogs; up to 2 caps fed to very large dogs). Horses can be fed a handful of cut and sifted herb daily in a mash.

Homeopathic Euphrasia is *an immediate healer for injuries to the eye!* Give the pellets orally, under the tongue or dissolve in water and dose to dogs. You can put the pellets into a piece of apple for a horse. Use homeopathics in small doses every 15 minutes for acute conditions, 3 times a day for older problems.

FENNEL, *Foeniculum vulgare,* is a Carminative and anti-Spasmodic for the digestive tract and intestines that can stimulate the appetite in horses, humans and dogs. It reduces "gassiness", prevents flatulent colic in horses and makes the gas that is passed less smelly. It can increase the flow of milk in lactating mothers. It relaxes the respiratory tract and is expectorant.

I feed powdered Fennel Seed in horses' feed - 1 tablespoon per meal per horse. A pinch in a dog's food at each meal works and a tea brewed from the whole seeds helps people, even children.

Fennel is a sweet, pungent herb that can be added to food and the plant can be found at Markets to add fresh to salads and stews. Stomach pain caused by gas is relieved right away by Fennel tea.

FENUGREEK, *Trigonella foenum-graecum,* is one of the oldest medicinal plants and is used for humans, horses and dogs. Fenugreek has profound blood sugar balancing properties but should only be used by insulin-dependent diabetics with supervision of a health care practitioner. It is also a uterine stimulant so is NOT to be used during pregnancy.

The seeds are used as a culinary herb in Middle Eastern cooking and are sprouted for a delicious addition to salads. Fenugreek seeds are fed to horses as a digestive aid and to balance weight gain (it is adaptogenic - will help stabilize the body). It is considered for all types of inflammation and for stomach pain. Added to a poultice it helps remove infections and swelling. It will increase milk flow when fed to lactating mothers. Fenugreek is a good choice for horses with Cushings Disease that are hard crested and prone to laminitis (the bloodsugar balancing effect). Horses are fed a tablespoon once daily; dogs would receive a 325 mg. capsule every other day; people would take the capsule once or twice daily.

A Fenugreek infusion makes a wonderful tonic rinse for the skin. It has a very distinctive aroma - I remember its smell from my childhood. It was an addition to a vitamin supplement that I fed to my horses in West Virginia!

FLAXSEEDS, *Linium usitatissimum*, are a nourishing herb that is used for humans, horses, dogs, cats, cattle, llamas, you name it! The seeds contain 40% fixed oil, linoleic, linolenic and oleic acids, mucilage, protein and linamarin. The oil (edible, coldpressed flaxseed oil) is used as a daily supplement to strengthen and heal the lungs, heart, digestive tract, skin and mucus membranes. The seeds can be cooked into "linseed / flaxseed jelly" to be fed to horses (the raw seeds can colic a horse - they release gases) or ground into a meal.

Whole seeds can be added to breads, muffins, salads, cookies, soups and such for people. The oil can be fed 2 to 3 times a week to small animals - from 1/2 teaspoon to the little guys, to 2 tablespoons for a very large dog. The oil or jelly (recipe below) will lubricate the digestive tract maintaining gut motility. If the bowels become too loose, you are feeding too much; just reduce the dose. This is also true with magnesium and vitamin C - dose to "bowel tolerance". If you create diarrhea, you have overdosed the nutrient.

For people you can brew a tea (infusion) with 3 teaspoons of seed, pour one cup of boiling water over the herb, steep for 20 minutes and drink, strained.

Flax will strengthen the lungs, break up congestion, soothe the throat and sinuses, heal skin from inside, help the heart and nourish hair when eaten or drunk as tea.

As a poultice, cooked flaxseeds will draw out infection and pain. It is useful for boils, psoriasis and shingles.

Flaxseed Jelly: For each horse use one handful of seeds and 2 quarts of water. Soak the seeds overnight (for 8 hours). Then bring to a boil, watching constantly! If this mixture boils over, and it tends to, it will make a gooey mess. Use a non-metal or enameled pot and wooden spoon. Stir often. Boil for a full hour. You will have reduced the water considerably and have a thick, slimey jelly to add directly to a bran mash or hard feed of grain or pellets. Do not strain it (you can't!). Dogs love to lick the pot/spoon and it's good for them; cats, too. It can help keep hairballs from forming in felines. Feed the jelly 2 to 3 times a week. It will help a horse shed and reduce dry, shedding hair in dogs. If you cook jelly for dogs, use the proportions above and keep the jelly in the fridge, feed a dog from one to three tablespoons of jelly in the food. People will not like to eat the jelly. It will keep for a week refrigerated.

FRANKINCENSE, *Boswellia thurifereB,* a resin tapped from a tree in East Africa and Arabia. It is used for pain as *Boswellia,* usually in powdered form placed into capsules and taken orally. The essential oil of Frankincense is used in Aromatherapy to support courage in people and animals.

The essential oil is a profound healer of skin and mouth infections - even having been used to treat Leprosy. It is antiseptic and a stimulant, applied full strength externally to old sores and dry infections; used in a carrier oil (grapeseed or olive) mixed half and half for new sores or irritations. Weeping, hot infections respond best to sandalwood oil and honey with systemic support through oral supplementation of anti-infection herbs. It has great therapeutic properties used directly on tumors under the skin (the skin is permeable, allowing the oil to reach the cancer.

GARLIC *Allium sativum,* is the supreme "antiseptic" herb, used internally to treat any infectious dis-ease in horses, dogs and people. Externally, garlic disinfects wounds and eliminates parasites. There have been warnings about garlic's detrimental effect upon one's liver when ingested and certainly, *in excess* of dose and frequency, the liver will be stressed by garlic (and by most pungent, oily or disinfecting foods) and some individuals will be extra sensitive. Use the herbalists' safety ways - dose just a little at first and watch for reactions.

Garlic can be made into an infused oil to rub into mange, lice or fungal infestations on the skin. This oil can be dropped into the ears for infections and to repel parasites. Garlic cloves, peeled, are used to infuse the oil and the cloves with greens can be boiled in water within a covered pot to create a safe insecticide spray for plants!

To feed garlic, peel and mince the raw clove and give one to four cloves per day to a horse; one eigth clove to a small dog up to one half clove for a very large dog per day (only dose a dog for 10 to 14 days, then rest him for 30 days and dose again if necessary). A human can eat one clove per day raw as a preventative and up to 3 cloves a day for 3 days as a treatment for infections (fevers, pulmonary disease, arthritis, digestive parasites and infections, blood disorders). These statements have not been approved by the FDA and we advise consulting your Holistic Veterinarian or natural health care practitioner about all remedies.

A single, peeled clove of garlic can be inserted into a horse's rectum to relieve pinworms. It will be pushed out with the next bowel movement. My grandmother was a midwife and "medicine woman" from a century ago and she used the same pinworm remedy for people.

Powdered or flaked, dry garlic can be fed mixed into animal foods and the liberal use of garlic to season our human dishes helps boost our good health. Eating fresh parsley will help deodorize the effects. Give small animals just a pinch, large dogs get a half teaspoon and horses receive a tablespoon per day.

All of my horses have eaten whole, raw garlic cloves right from my hand. They sense the good medicine of garlic. If your horse doesn't like garlic, mix it well into something he likes or use garlic supplements or garlic salt.

Do not feed the salt to dogs. If your dog's nose gets crusty and "mushroom-like", it is likely caused by excess salt, so examine his or her diet for sodium.

Feeding garlic can help repel biting insects because the sulfur from the herb is released in the sweat or skin oils. The best way I have found to cook with garlic is to roast the whole bulbs in the oven at 375 degrees for 15 minutes or so, then freeze them. I can pop out the roasted cloves to add to dishes any time.

GINGER, *Zingiber officinale,* can be a warming and healing herb for our horses and ourselves. I make ginger tea with a few slices of fresh ginger root simmered in a pan of pure water. It tastes wonderful as is or with some honey (honey and lemon added will soothe a cold or flu). This tea served plain can stop nausea and dizziness.

A strong brew of ginger tea can be added to a hot bath to warm the core (of an adult human) and stimulate circulation - use this with caution, though. If you use too much ginger or the water is too hot, you can over stimulate the circulatory system!

Powdered ginger root is added by the teaspoon to a horse's wet, warm bucket feed on a cold night to support the digestion and warm the body. This also has a clearing effect on the lungs. I use one spoonful for a small horse; two spoons for a large horse.

Ginger root capsules or crystalized ginger pieces can be carried to take in case of motion sickness (in humans). For dogs with motion sickness, I generally give homeopathic Cocculus indicus.

Essential oil of ginger root can be placed (a drop or two) onto a tissue that is carried to "sniff" if one is feeling nauseous. Peppermint oil helps in this way as well. Both of these oils are counter-indicated for pregnancy. And, ginger is too strong to use for cats in any form.

GINSENGS are adaptogenic herbs; meaning that they exhibit both calming and stimulating properties depending upon the needs of the body.

Korean Ginseng is Panax schinseng
Siberian Ginseng is Eleutheroccocus
Wild American is Panax quinquefolium

The ROOT is used for Horses, Dogs and Humans to combat stress, *support the circulatory sytem*, to aid physical strength and recovery from distress, it *fights fatigue*, calms the nervous system and helps with mental clarity.

Rich in B vitamins (the premier nerve support and healing vitamin complex!), selenium, vitamins A, C and E (anti-oxidants); Ginseng is a nourisher of the body's DNA and RNA. Ginsengs contain ginsenosides, glycosides, sterols and volatile oils. Ginseng can lower blood sugar levels, can anti-dote some toxins, protect tissues from radiation and enhance the health of sex organs.

You can find Ginseng as an ingredient in many supplements for animals and people. If you supplement it by itself, start with small amounts and adjust as needed - it is a potent and pricey herb that is well worth its cost when it is needed! It can be fed as a dry, ground herb in the food or as a decoction; cooked into a tea.

GOLDENSEAL,*Hydrastis canadensis,* is an herbal "anti-biotic" used to treat infections of all types. An herbal combination used for Conjunctivitis, irritations, removing debris and blocked tear ducts for horses, dogs and people is made with the leaf (root is too strong!!). The tincture of root and leaf is used on infected wounds. The leaf or root can be brewed into a tea for ingestion (it is bitter) to treat systemic infection.

To make the eyewash, combine equal parts goldenseal leaf and Rose Petals and store in an airtight container. For eyewash, steep one tablespoonful in two cups of pure water just off the boil for 20 minutes. Cool, strain VERY well and add a pinch of sea salt to make it isotonic. This wash can be used twice daily for up to 10 days. Use dried rose petals from an herbalist that are not contaminated by any chemicals.

GOTU KOLA, *Centella asiatica,*In Sanskrit, Gotu Kola is called *brahmi* (Brahma means cosmic consciousness). Its leaf looks like the 2 hemispheres of the brain and its action is upon brain function - tissue, memory, etc. I have a lot of experience with this herb. After a fall from my Eventer over a ditch jump in the '70's, I had a severe concussion and drank Gotu Kola tea every hour while my brother kept me awake reading to me. It is decongestant, aids circulation and is calming.

A friend actually grew "tons" of Gotu Kola in her green house and would bring giant bags of the fresh herb for me to feed to a laminitic mare and it really helped her. While working at a rescue facility, we had a mare brought in who was blind and held her head tilted all the time - I connected with her and read her field, discovering that someone had beaten her on the head. I started her on Gotu Kola and she began improving. She eventually held her head straighter and her eyesight began to return. I also fed her Vitamin B2 (riboflavin) and cod liver oil for her eyes.

A friend who drag raced a Harley (nitro-fueled motorcycle with 2 engines!) wrecked many years ago and had a serious concussion. He took Gotu Kola and we felt that it helped during his very long recovery.

Gotu Kola tea is relaxing, not a stimulant, but it enhances brain function, so it makes you feel better and more productive. I love the taste of the fresh herb and of tea from the dried leaves. I used to make huge salads with it when Cathie brought bags of it. That was a time when I truly felt my most clear headed! Gotu Kola is a profound "memory herb".

Too high a dose can cause headaches and aggravate itching. Do not exceed 1000 milligrams daily or 4 cups of tea per day unless advised by a practitioner.

HAWTHORN BERRY, *Crayeagus oxyacantha*, is an adaptogen, an herb that equalizes or *balances* the system it works upon. It resonates with the heart and circulatory system, being able to lower or raise blood pressure to normal levels. It strengthens blood vessels, dilates them, regulates heart beat, helps digest fats, improves the heart's pumping action, improves local circulation and is used for angina.

Hawthorn Berry syrup, decoctions, capsules and tinctures can be found in health food stores.

Hawthorn berry capsules daily stopped the breaking of blood vessels in my Mother's eyes. A friend lowered his very high blood pressure with an herbal combination based on Hawthorn Berry. Another friend controls his heart rhythm with Hawthorn. I know a horse whose heart murmur was eased by it.

Herbs should not be mixed with pharmaceuticals without the advise of a Practitioner. Many herbs like Hawthorn can replace the chemicals that come with side effects.

I feed the whole dried berries in a bucket feed for horses, 10 to 12 berries for a large horse. The herbal capsules can be given to dogs, 325 to 475 mg. cap once daily for a medium size dog.

HEMP - *Cannabis satvia* is "Hemp" and is used for making rope, textiles and the like. *Cannabis indica* is also "Hemp" and has been used for medicinal purposes for centuries.

HEMP SEED is almost 50% HEMP OIL which contains 80% essential fatty acids! The nourishing seeds are a very digestible protein source; containing a more complete amino acid structure than meat, soy or dairy products. Hemp seed and oil are *full* of Omega 3's, essential minerals and contain no gluten.

Hemp seeds (usually slightly "ground") can be added to yogurt, to cereals, toppings for crackers or chips, etc. Cooking will destroy nutrients - and the seeds should be stored in the refrigerator (oil, also). Horses can be fed up to a quarter cup daily (it *is* pricey, so a teaspoon now and then can suffice!) and dogs would get just a pinch daily. People can use the Hemp seed oil as a salad dressing; added to cottage cheese and so on. The nutritional "punch" it will give to any diet is well worth the cost. Hemp seeds and the hemp seed oil can be found in health food markets and should be in the refrigerated section.

Hemp seeds and the oil are edible for all species (they are added to most bird seed mixes to boost nutrients) and nourish the skin from within - can heal eczema - as well as being anti-inflammatory. Hemp seed oil is used in topical skin moisturizers and massage oils.

"Medical" Cannabis is effectively used to strengthen brain cells and in Alzheimer's treatment. It stops vomiting, increases appetite, eases nausea and decreases pressure in the eye ball. It makes an ointment for topical use that stops pain and itching that other treatments have failed to control.

Cannabidiol from Cannabis has been shown to inhibit cancer cells and stop metastasis!

A recipe for the healing ointment (that can be made in countries or states where the use of medical cannabis is legal!) was taught to me decades ago (when the herb actually was legal here) by a friend who had run a spike through the bone of her finger; pulled it out and healed the wound with this salve! I personally knew it to soothe a horse whose face had been sutured back together and the pain and itching were intolerable until we rescued him with this:

Slowly warm 1 large tablespoon of organic herb into 1 cup of oil (olive oil is perfect - sunflower or safflower are good) in a double boiler or a small enameled or glass pot set into a larger pot of simmering water. Keep the water topped up and warm the mixture for 45 minutes to an hour. Strain oil while hot and immediately place a half ounce of pure beeswax into the oil, stirring until it melts. Pour into a jar (glass is best) right away and let cool. All of these ingredients are healing in their own right and the cannabis stops the pain and itch.

HOPS, *Humulus lupulus,* flowers are used as a calmative in many herbal blends for people and for horses. This is because they are very effective! Hops are used to make beer, of course, and in many stables, a bottle of dark beer was added to a warm mash for a horse who was anxious or had worked so hard he needed help relaxing that evening. If added while the wet mash was quite hot (before cooling to feed), the alcohol evaporated!

In Herbology, Hops are used to relax the nerves, as an appetite stimulant (beer works this way because of the Hops), as a digestive aid to the gall bladder (horses do not have gallbladders), liver (*without* alcohol which is detrimental to the liver!) and to relieve gas - for these purposes, the flowers are steeped in water as an infusion, or tea; or are fed soaked in water, a small handful daily for a large horse for no more than 7 days (small amounts in treats and such can be fed longer).

Hops are not used for dogs because the herb can *cause depression* and the smaller size of canines predisposes them to this effect - hops are more potent for them. And because of this characteristic, Hops are not recommended for children nor for adult people who are depressed or susceptible to depression. If you drink beer and feel more "down" because of it, the hops are most likely the cause.

Hops have Phosphorus, Potassium, Vitamins C and B complex in high amounts. The tea for humans has been used for earaches, headaches, gas, itching, neuralgia, dizziness and insomnia.

I grew a wonderful big Hops vine by my front door on Furnace Street when I had the Zen Center. It started as a tiny twig from a seed catalog and made copious blooms that attracted beneficial insects and made soothing, fresh tea!

JUNIPER, *Juniperus communis*, over a decade ago, my Appaloosa, Breath of Snow, developed a raw tumor on his sheath that quickly grew to the size of her fist. My Vet surgically removed it. It returned in 6 months, was removed again by the Vet. It returned again, was surgically excised and the Vet said there was so much scar tissue that another surgery would not be possible. As the tumor was growing back, I made the "Anti-tumor Spray" (developed from my long experience with herbal properties) and began spraying the growth many times throughout each day. The tumor shrank and finally disappeared.

It has been used by Veterinarians and was sold by an herbalist in New Mexico who had taken my healing classes at our University.

 RECIPE: Add one very large handful of Chamomile blossoms and one big handful of **Juniper Berries** to a bottle of dark red wine in a non-metal (glass or enameled) cooking pot. Boil, covered for a half hour then let stand, covered for 8 hours. Strain and apply to skin/growths several times per day. This is a remedy for people, horses and dogs. We have not used it on cats, so we have no experience to know if it is safe for felines. The Chamomile pulls things away from the body (remember that a wet Chamomile tea bag will draw out splinters!).

KOMBU, *Laminaria japonica*, is a "Sea Weed" with amazing medicinal properties. Kombu is harvested off of the coasts of Japan and contains a host of Vitamins, abundant Minerals, Trace Elements and Glutamic Salts. It is used in cooking to add flavor, nourishment and to aid the softening of dry beans and reduce gasses.

It is purchased as a dried vegetable and can be added "as is" to soups, stews, vegetables and in salads as a dry crumble (or soaked in water briefly). Soaked Kombu is fed to dogs for arthritis - 2 to 4 grams daily (about one half to three quarters of a "strip") for a large dog, 1 to 3 grams daily for medium dogs and 1/2 to 1 gram for a small pooch. 3 grams of Kombu has the total amount of the necessary mineral, Iodine, for a human being per day. Iodine is needed for endocrine, glandular, lymphatic health and to maintain healthy skin, hair, nails, claws, hooves, etc.

I have used Kombu (well soaked and softened in pure water) as a wound dressing held on with plastic film/wrap (to maintain the moisture) and an outer "Vetrap" bandage. I have applied this to many an Equine injury, including those that needed sutures but they either kept pulling out or could not be used. The healing is remarkable and scarring is minimal. I used this on a severe cut to my hand when I could not afford to have it stitched. The Iodine content makes it antiseptic and stimulating and the other minerals support cutaneous restructuring.

LAVENDER , *Lavendula officinalis,* is of the most popular medicinal herbs since ancient times, it is the supreme calming, soothing plant for our horses, our dogs and our families. Use it with confidence. It is non-toxic, rarely an allergin and easy to distinguish from other plants. If you or an animal are pregnant, do not use Lavender (or other herbs without consulting a Practitioner). It can be a uterine stimulant.

Lavender can be used as an infusion, a tincture, an ointment, a cream or as essential oil. The flowers can be dried and used in pillows or sachets to induce calm and aid sleep. They can be added to teas and to lemonade for flavor and calming.

Essential oil of Lavender is the most important ingredient in a natural first aid kit. It is used for calming, on acupoints, on wounds full strength, on burns (including sunburn) when added to aloe gel, on rashes in a carrier oil, full strength on insect bites and rubbed on the soles of the feet for shock and anxiety.

Lavender oil added to massage oils will help nourish the skin and relax the muscles. Lavender makes an excellent chest rub for congestion. It can be combined with peppermint oil to rub into painful joints (contra-pregnancy!). You can put 10 drops into an ounce of water in a spray bottle to scent the air, spray into your animal's coat to condition it. A stronger spray will repel lice and fleas. Lavender oil can be used for all animals with the exception of cats.

MEADOWSWEET, *Filependula ulmaria*, smells so good, I love to just *inhale* from the bag of dried herb and imagine real meadows and horses grazing and how their breath would be scented...Full of salicylic acid and the related compounds spiraeine and gaultherin it is a profound anti-rheumatic and anti-inflammatory remedy. Because

19

Meadowsweet also contains tannins and essential oils it acts to protect the stomach, soothe mucus membranes, reduce acidity and ease nausea.

The dried leaves and flowers are used in infusions (teas) for people and dogs; tinctures for people; and can be fed directly to horses for inflammation, pain, arthritis and digestive disturbances. Meadowsweet is not to be fed to cats because of the salicylic acid! It is "aspirin-like". Because it is healing to gastric and peptic ulcers, it is a gentle choice for pain relief in those suffering from ulcers.

Meadowsweet is a mild remedy for diarrhea as a tea for children, given in small amounts. For arthritic horses I add a small handful to their bran mashes or hard feed. It is helpful with Laminitis and does not damage the stomach as some pain control meds can. Of course, Meadowsweet is also not as strong as the allopathic medicines for pain. In situations where it is necessary to relieve severe or prolonged pain, we must use the chemicals to be humane and then look at management possibilities down the road that could substitute or include appropriate herbs.

MILK THISTLE, *Carduus marianus*, seeds are the supreme liver support and healing herb. We add 2 tablespoons of dried seeds to the bucket feed once daily for a horse with liver stress. For dogs, we give a 325 mg. capsule to a medium size dog once daily.

I have seen milk thistle cleanse the damaged liver of a gelding in his 20's who had been dosed repeatedly with Ivermectin wormer until he jaundiced (mucous membranes turned yellow).

MULLEIN, *Verbascum thapsus*, is a powerful pulmonary healer, used for cough (kennel cough), pneumonia, pleuritis, bronchitis, tuberculosis and asthma. It is also used for diarrhea, bleeding of the bowels and cramps. The dried downy leaves are used in an infusion - one handful to a pint of water. The tea must be well strained and the fluffy down shouldn't be allowed into your eyes or inhaled while handling the dry herb. Mullein is also infused into oil (olive or sunflower) to use warm in the ears of dogs, horses and humans for ache or infection (garlic is added to the mixture). If you do ear coning (with hollow candles of linen/cotton and beeswax), Mullein oil dropped into the ears an hour before coning softens the ear wax and sooths the tissues - Do not ear cone animals - it takes too much time and the flame is spooky.

Mullein can be purchased in health food stores as the dry, cut and sifted herb or as infused ear oil already prepared. Give the tea/infusion to a dog with a dropper or small syringe by mouth slowly, a couple of tablespoons at a time every hour for coughing. Dose a horse with a large syringe (60cc catheter tip syringe works well), one to two ounces (30 to 60 cc's) every hour for a cough. Humans drink a cup of tea every hour.

NETTLES, *Uritica dioica*, are an incredible tonic herb, *full* of nutrition and medicinal properties. They contain formic acid, histamine, acetylchlorine, iron, silica, many minerals because they pull them from deep in the soil, glucoquinones, tannins, vitamin A and the water soluble vitamins B complex and C. They prevent scurvy (a vitamin C deficiency syndrome), clear uric acid from the body to relieve gout and arthritis and are astringent and can stop bleeding.

The histamine and formic acid cause the "sting" which is painful, so harvest Nettles with thick gloves and long sleeves. Dry the leaves thoroughly before use. Fresh Nettle stalks were used for "urtication" - flogging of paralyzed limbs to stimulate the nerves. It is more appropriate these days to infuse vegetable oil with Nettle leaf and rub it into the limbs.

Nettles are tonic and nutritious. They increase energy by adding needed minerals that enrich the blood. They are a circulatory stimulant, lower blood pressure and feed the skin, hair, nails and hooves. Nettles will put "dapples" on your horses' coats and will make your skin glow, your hair grow. The ointment is used for hemorrhoids.

The tea/infusion made from the dried Nettles tastes wonderful, doesn't need sweetening. It is a profound health tonic and helps clear the skin from within. I feed a hand full of dried leaves in a horse's bucket feed often.

Nettles have been used for centuries by many cultures. They truly prove than one man's weed is another man's medicine. Nettle leaf tea bags are easy to find in health food stores.

OATSTRAW, *Avena sativa*, is the "stem" or straw of the oat plant which is a grassy herb grown for its sweet, nutrient rich seeds (oats). The Oat Straw of the plant has soothing, calmitive properties for all animals and people. It is a mild and benign herb (unless one has an allergy to oats) that is usually safe for youngsters. It builds the immune system, supports digestion, is healing to the nerves and skin and loosens tension in the body.

To gain these effects, the oatstraw should be brewed as a tea or *infusion* - for HORSES, use two large handfuls to 2 quarts of water just off the boil. Let this steep for half an hour then strain and give to the horse as a tea to drink or poured over his ration. The water releases the active compounds and suspends them so the body can absorb and utilize the calming effect when ingested.

For DOGS the tea can be made with one tablespoon herb to 2 cups of water, then give 1/4 cup to a small dog, 1/2 cup to a large dog.

People can drink the tea from a teaspoon of herb in a tea ball or bag to one cup of water. This is great before bedtime.

For horses, the calming Oatstraw tea is not going to "test" at competitions where more sedative herbs and compounds are forbidden. Oat HAY still has the oats (seeds) and is fed - Oat STRAW is the stem after oat harvest.

The Oatstraw herb can be found at health food stores and herbalists where it is very pure and in a chopped form. If any being gets loose bowels or has any swelling or trouble breathing - these may be signs of an allergic reaction. Contact your health care practitioner (and cease use of the allergen).

OLIVE LEAF, *Olea europaea*, is an incredible immune system booster and healer for people, horses and dogs. Olive leaf extracts, powders and gels can be found as supplements in Veterinary supply catalogs for dogs and for horses. Any health food store or herb shop will have the supplements for humans. I buy the powder and cap it for myself and my dogs and feed it in mashes to my horses. I give one capsule to my small dog daily, 2 capsules to the large dog when needed. For the horses, I add 2 tablespoons daily per horse if they are fighting something or just 1 spoon if they were exposed to something like a virus or bacteria.

Olive Leaf is anti-fungal, anti-viral and anti-bacterial. It is one of the highest antioxidant containing foods available and is known to have strong anti-parasite properties. I have used Olive Leaf Extract for my own bronchitis, for intestinal flu for a friend, for a dog with bacterial diarrhea and horses with respiratory tract infections, a urinary tract infection, to support the body in healing a septic leg wound, orally to help with an eye infection and for a colt prone to worm infestations. I found it to be effective each time.

The properties of Olive Leaf support the entire metabolism - by inhibiting pathogenic (disease causing) microbes and parasites, it allows the body a return to its own strong defense system. It works on the causes of a disorder, not just the symptoms. This means that the disorder won't simply return (perhaps stronger) after the "medicine" is stopped.

OREGON GRAPE ROOT, *Mahonia aquafolium*, is an herb that can be used as a substitute for the over-harvested Goldenseal. Both are "herbal anti-biotics" and contain the alkaloids *hydrastine* and *berberine*. The berries of Oregon Grape are used to reduce fevers and are made into jelly, but the Root is the medicinal part. I make Oregon Grape Root Tincture by placing 4 tablespoons root (dried/cut and sifted) into 8 ounces of pure water and 8 ounces of pure ingestible alcohol (Vodka). I place the bottle in a warm spot, sealed (it needs to be a glass container with tight seal). Several times daily I shake the mixture. After 2 weeks, I strain it into dark bottles, squeezing the liquid out of the herbs.

Tinctures last for many years. You can put the drops into a cup of very warm water to evaporate the alcohol for animals and children. Use 30 drops of tincture twice daily for adult humans; 10 drops for children with approval from a practitioner; 5 to 10 drops for a dog and brew a decoction with a handful of herb in water, strain and put the "tea" into a bran mash for a horse.

Oregon Grape Root as a tincture or simmered in water as a decoction will cleanse and strengthen the LIVER, SPLEEN and GALL BLADDER (horses do not have gall bladders, but they have spleens and livers. The equine liver secretes bile directly into the digestive system).

For people it can heal the liver "chi" imbalances such as anger, headaches, poor digestion and blood toxins. Oregon Grape is a good blood purifier. We often use this herb when an infection has set in, systemically, to boost the immune-system response and "fight" the bacteria or even virus. For gall bladder "attacks" in people, we have used the decoction, sipped all through the day during a water fast (nothing else but pure water) for 3 days, then the tablespoon of extra virgin olive oil with lemon juice taken each morning as easily digested foods are added.

PAPAYA, *Carica papaya*, the fruit of the Papaya is used for digestive health - to *maintain it* and to *return to it*! Full of enzymes (papain), vitamins and minerals, the delicious Papaya can heal ulcers when fed to humans and horses. You can purchase the fruit fresh, dried or canned and its properties are intact in all 3 forms. It is used for diarrhea, to soothe the intestinal tract, for protein digestion and as a blood cleanser.

The juice squeezed from the fruit can be used on wounds and is very effective to prevent and to control "proud flesh". This is a condition where the granulation of tissue as a wound heals is happening faster at the interior than the healing of the skin to cover the wound!

I keep dried Papaya Fruit strips (or chewable tablets) to eat at night if I wake up with "heartburn". Instead of drinking some bicarbonate of soda in water (which does relieve the burning, but compromises the hydrochloric/digesting acids of the stomach), I just chew on the papaya, drink a bit of water and fall back to sleep.

Horses are very susceptible to the development of ulcers. Stress is the usual cause along with an unnatural diet of grains and their by-products. Signs of an ulcer can range from regular colic episodes to bucking when ridden or just refusing to move. Horses respond to pain in a variety of ways and ulcers are very painful. Papaya does not just cover up the symptoms, it can actually heal the ulceration - but, the causes of the stress and imbalance must be addressed!

The blood cleansing properties of papaya also lend it to helping with allergies.

Dogs with digestive disorders usually respond best to the addition of pure pumpkin in their diet - canned, without the milk and spices for pie! Cats respond well to added Colostrum powder in their food. If you suspect infection or parasites in any being's digestive tract, Papaya can help (Colloidal silver and goldenseal are also good choices, but consult with your holistic health practitioner on these).

PAU D' ARCO, inner bark from South America is an anti-tumor herb that is also used for yeast and fungal infections. The best way to prepare it is to make a decoction by simmering the bark in pure water for 20 minutes. Use non-metal pots and utensils and cover the simmering brew. Let it stand covered for another 20 minutes after simmering. Strain and use or refrigerate for future uses.

The decoction is given internally to people, horses and dogs to fight candida/yeast infection or overgrowth and to slow the growth of and eliminate tumors. *To make the decoction for* DOGS: use 2 tablespoons bark in 4 cups of water. Give the brew in the food once daily - 1/4 cup liquid for dogs over 100 lbs.; 3 tbsp. for large dogs; 2 tbsp. medium; 1tbsp. small and a teaspoon for very tiny dogs.

For Horses: brew 2 big handfuls of bark in 3 quarts of water as above. Give 1 to 2 cups of liquid daily depending upon the size of the horse. You can feed the cut and sifted bark directly in the horse's food; about 2 tablespoons daily.

People can simmer a teaspoon of bark in a 1 1/2 cups water to make a cup of "tea" to drink each day.

The proven properties of Pau D'Arco are tumor reducing, system balancing effects that are useful with internal and external growths. By drinking the decoction, these properties work with the body's immune system to encapsulate and isolate the tumor, thus starving it which reduces and eventually eliminates it. Yeasts are also reduced by an enzyme-like action that "explodes" the spores and they no longer grow.

PEPPERMINT, *Mentha spp./M. Piperite,* relaxes the the muscles of the digestive tract and stimulates bile production so it is a great choice for indigestion, flatulence, colic and nausea. The volatile oils in peppermint contain menthol, so it can be a profound pain reliever and decongestant. Peppermint leaves are used in infusions (teas) and can be made into a tincture, used in liniments, vaporizers or infused into oils like grapeseed (do not use any grape products for dogs - it can damage their kidneys - no raisins, etc.). Mint can stimulate the liver and the uterus, so it is contraindicated for pregnancy. It is too strong for babies of any species (use spearmint, it is milder).

Essential oil of peppermint is very cooling. Try it in a spray bottle: one pint water with 20 drops oil, for a cooling skin spray in the Summer. If you use strong green tea instead of plain water, it will also be a safe sunscreen spray.

The scent or flavor of Peppermint will antidote (nullify) homeopathic medicines, so wait an hour before or after its use to dose the medicine.

PSYLLIUM, *Plantago ovate,* seeds and the hulls of the seeds (or "husks") are used for people, horses and dogs (less often for dogs because of the fast way meat moves through the canine gut) to cleanse the intestinal tract by ingestion. For humans, bulking fiber and roughage are often missing from typical modern diets in some countries - adding healthy vegetable fiber like psyllium can change a person's life.

Psyllium products are used in people to help heal ulcers, constipation, colitis and to eliminate toxins and very old fecal matter from the large intestine and colon. There are proprietary products with psyllium at the market and pharmacy. Be sure to read ingredients; psyllium and real sugar will be acceptable for humans and animals... chemical bulking agents and artificial sweeteners could cause poisoning. For human OTC products, follow the directions and be sure to drink lots of pure water through the day. You can take the pure psyllium in capsules with lots of water. Daily fiber is essential to a person's body health - you *can* also provide that fiber with fresh vegetables, whole grains and fruits.

Health food stores and herbal supplies will have 100% psyllium, which is much better than mixed products. You feed half to one third as much pure psyllium as you do the products with all the sugar.

Equine Sand Colic prevention:

Horses that graze, eat off of sandy areas or are feed from the ground directly need monthly feeding of psyllium to work the sand out of their guts (the cecum collects it) and maintain motility. Sand can completely block the digestive tract (sand impaction) and kill a horse.

Feed horses one ounce twice daily for one week of the 100% psyllium;

or 3 ounces twice daily of the OTC product w/sugar for a week every month.

Put the herb into a feed of wheat bran, grain (that the horse is used to getting) or pellets; *mix well* and *soak* it all with water.

Dogs can get things stuck in their systems (shards from cooked bones, pieces of wood or metal or..?) that need to be safely eliminated. The dog will likely get diarrhea to try to slip the object on through. I took a dog to my Vet with diarrhea after he had eaten a pinecone. The Tech freaked out when I listed psyllium as one of the things I had done for him. The Veterinarian came in and told her why that had been a *good* thing to do. My dog was fine, but I'm not suggesting anyone else diagnose or prescribe - just telling a story here.

I find regular feeding of canned, PLAIN pumpkin to be the best canine bowel regulator (no spices included for pie making); fed a tablespoon daily up to 3 tbsp for big dogs.

Psyllium Seed is an inexpensive, safe (when plenty of water is provided and when there are no underlying chronic diseases or bloody stool) method to detox and cleanse the body, even to regulate one's weight by dumping the sludge that clings to the lining of the digestive tract (this interferes with proper digestion).

PURSLANE, *Portulaceae sativa*, is a blood cooling and blood cleansing plant with succulent characteristics that grows in moist places. When I lived on the Organic Herb Farm commune, we grew purslane and ate it in salads, used it as healing fodder for the animals and sold it at the market.

It's fat, fleshy leaves are full of moisture and minerals pulled from deep in the soil. It has an unusual, almost salty flavor and is great with big green salads with fruits added (blueberries, mango, orange slices, etc.). Nuts and seeds will add even more, highly digestable minerals. These foods will nourish the blood and bone.

Always use herbs like Purslane from clean sources (no chemical pesticides or fertilizers used!) and take a little from a lot (leave some behind for others and the Earth).

RASPBERRY, *Rubus ideates*, is the premiere herb for female health of all species and is especially useful during pregnancies. That being said, we MUST state that a health care practitioner is necessary to evaluate the safe use of any herb during pregnancy!

Raspberry leaf herb, dried, is fed cut and sifted to mares (horses) or made into an infusion (a tea) that is poured over a mash. The herb strengthens the uterine wall and is used for urinary tract health and support. It prevents retained placenta/afterbirth and is tonic to the reproductive organs before conception and after giving birth. Herbalists feed it during the entire pregnancy.

Dogs are fed red raspberry leaf, usually included from a pinch to a tablespoon (depending upon weight) in each meal to support the uterine health, liver health and renal health.

People benefit from red raspberry leaf and fruit. The infusion of the leaf helps with menstrual cramps, excessive menstrual flow and bloating. The delicious fruits are equally effective during one's period to balance the body and the emotions. Both forms are also treatments for diarrhea and strengthen the uterine and renal systems.

RED CLOVER, *Trifolium pretense*, is an acne fighting, liver cleansing, blood purifying blossom that is used for treating cancer because of its effect on protein assimilation. The blossoms should be steeped in pure water just off the boil because actually boiling the herb will destroy many of its beneficial properties. This infusion or "tea" can be taken, a cup at a time (it is a sweet, earthy drink) 4 times a day for the human. Adding honey helps for weakness and for stomach disorders or cancers.

Red Clover is high in *Calcium, Magnesium and Potassium*. This makes it a good tea to drink at the end of the day if you have *muscle cramps during the night*. We drank Nettle tea in the mornings and Red Clover at night when I lived on the organic herb farm, everyone had the most gorgeous skin and hair!

I have used Red Clover tea brewed for dogs with tumors and had success in reducing them. I drank it as a teenager along with taking 50,000 IU of Vitamin A daily for my serious acne (had a stressful youth).

Red Clover "cut and sifted" (dry blossoms) can be fed to horses, one handful daily and is generally used in cancer treatment for the equine. It will support the healing of skin disorders from internally - such as rainrot, greasy heel, etc. (the addition of Calendula Blossoms is very helpful, too).

Red Clover has actually been used for Leprosy, to purify the blood and support cutaneous structures; strengthen nerves.

ROSE HIPS, *Rosa species,* are rich in vitamin C, A Rutin, selenium, manganese and B Complex vitamins. Rose hips can be fed whole or ground to horses in a bucket feed for stress, coughs, inflammation, infections and to support hoof health.

ROSEMARY, *Rosmarinus officinalis*, is a Mediterranean shrub with powerful medicinal properties. Use the infusion as a tonic for the scalp and the essential oil (mixed with a carrier oil like olive oil) for sores and dandruff. It is contraindicated for heart disorders as in the oil form or in strong doses it is a cardiac stimulant and can increase blood pressure.

The powdered or ground rosemary "leaves" are used on oozing or weeping sores, can be packed into wounds to act as an antiseptic "scab" while healing takes place rapidly beneath it. It is especially useful for wounds on horses.

The powder can be used alone or mixed with powdered thyme, sage and/or lavender to make a flea and tick repellent powder for dogs. Just brush it into their coats. It contains phenol which is toxic to cats.

SENNA, *Senna Alexandria*, Years ago, the owner of a boarding stable called me. A horse belonging to one of her clients had coliced. This mare had not had a bowel movement for five days! They were giving up; mineral oil tubings, Banamine (a drug used for colic in horses) and constant walking if she tried to roll had not helped the sweet mare.

The owner adored this horse. She was herself falling apart at the prospect of putting her "down". I said, "Try senna pods - soak a handful of dry pods in a pint of tepid water for 3 hours, then strain it and dose the liquid orally and just repeat it every hour." They did this and after 3 doses, the mare starting having bowel movements! She recovered. I received a beautiful card from the owner and one perfect manure "apple" sprayed with gold paint.

My immediate thoughts of Senna pods came from my past as an herbalist and from the old time medicines we used at my first stable. There was a kind of dark, grainy powder my Veterinarian prescribed and I used for impaction colic in horses that we mixed with warm water and dosed from a syringe into the horse's mouth. I remember that simply getting the liquid all over my skin would give me raging diarrhea - I also remembered always that the main ingredient in that magical powder was Senna Pod.

A human friend had tried lots of laxatives that had been prescribed by doctors and was getting more ill every day. I told him about the simple senna pods and he used 6 pods to a cup of warm water, drinking it every couple of hours until he had relief. After that, he drank a cup every morning.

Senna is not a good choice for those with high blood pressure or known anxiety issues - it can be stimulating to the whole metabolism. It does support peristalsis in the colon. It has saved several horses I've known personally that were in trouble with impaction colics. The dry pods can be found in health food stores.

SLIPPERY ELM, *Ulmus fulva,* the inner bark of Slippery Elm is used to heal diarrhea in people, horses, dogs, even cats. It will soothe inflamed tissues. A decoction will heal a sore throat, calm irritated skin and rashes; cool and relieve hemorrhoids (externally and by drinking the liquid) and help heal tumors both internal and external.

Slippery Elm is a premiere ulcer remedy, is high in protein and the B-complex vitamins and has small amounts of magnesium (the miraculous mineral for heart, lung, muscle, nerve and brain health).

It has been used for Asthma; Diarrhea and Constipation both (!); Renal Problems, Coughs and even Tuberculosis/Appendicitis/Pneumonia/Whooping Cough, some very serious conditions.

For horses, it can be fed powdered in a really wet mash to heal the digestive tract, lungs and kidneys/bladder. One quarter cup daily for 10 days can have remarkable results. For dogs, a teaspoon, up to one heaping tablespoon of the powdered bark added to soaked food once daily for 7 days is a common dose. Cats can have 1/2 to a full teaspoon if quite large, fed once a day for a week. You can simmer the bark for 20 minutes and feed the decoction to the animals. This liquid is best for humans, drink a cup full twice daily for 3 to 7 days.

Slippery Elm is used to make herbal tablets: equal amounts of the Slippery Elm powder and powdered herb are very lightly moistened with vegetable glycerin, rolled out into "ropes", cut into tablets and left to dry. This is very effective. The powder can also be packed into capsules.

THYME, *Thymus vulgaris* & *Thymus serpyllum*, I want to share with you an Herbal Combination for dogs. The dog in nature *does* eat plants - not only will he chew on grasses and herbs, but will eat the contents from the digestive tract of a "kill". Now, if he caught a rabbit for supper, the rabbit will have herbs and grasses in various stages of digestion that will become nourishment for the dog as well.

The properties of plants are vital to the good health of your dog and a combination that we use regularly, added to the dog's food (with a little water to connect it) is: *Equal parts powdered (ground) Thyme, powdered Parsley and Burdock Root powder.*

The Thyme is a digestive aid and "conditions" the digestive tract. It is a systemic anti-parasite remedy - thymol, the volatile oil in thyme, is anti-heartworm. Parsley cleanses and tones the renal system (bladder and kidneys) and strengthens the heart. Burdock supports and heals the liver, cleanses the endocrine system, balancing glands and hormones.

This supplement can be fed for up to 6 months at a time with a break of about 45 days to let the body regulate itself. A dog over 100 lbs. would get 3 teaspoons daily; 80lbs to 100 lbs. would get 2 tsps. daily; 40 lbs. to 80lbs. would get 1 tsp. daily and under 40lbs. would receive 1/2 tsp. daily (a really little mini-dog, give just a pinch).

TUMERIC, *Curcuma longa*, is a healer of inflammation, digestion and is a blood purifier. It is the root - or rhizome that is used. It is used in Curry (such a healthy addition to food!) and is taken in capsules to reduce pain from inflammation and arthritis; to normalize blood sugar levels; to relieve coughing and asthma; is anti-bacterial and anti-tumor!

I have fed Turmeric to horses with arthritis and to a gelding with melanomas. It was helpful in all these cases and I feel it improved and prolonged the high quality lives of my equine friends. It can be fed to horses with insulin imbalances as well and an equine dose ranges from 1 to 2 tablespoons (1/3 to 2/3 ounce) of the powdered (ground) herb twice daily.

Humans take 2 to 4 capsules after a meal to aid blood sugar normalization. Taken at bedtime, it can help reduce pain and detox the liver and gallbladder. Human use for tumor reduction has been practiced for centuries.

For dogs, a pinch in the food for little ones, up to a half teaspoon for a large dog is the usual dose.

You can make Turmeric paste to apply to bruises and swellings by mixing a handful of herb with a teaspoon of sea salt. Add water or milk until it forms a stiff paste to apply to the injury.

 Turmeric helps with the pain of chronic joint injuries, back pain, muscle tearing or bruising and helps support the liver (as most every yellow herb does).

UVA URSI, *Arctostaphylos uva-ursi,* is a supreme Urinary Tract inflammation remedy. Also called "Bearberry", it is diuretic and antibacterial with astringent/antiseptic properties that cleanse urine production. I make an infusion for people or dogs (a "cup of tea") to sip on throughout the day. I feed the dry leaves to horses - one handful in the morning and one handful in the evening feeds for 3 to 7 days.

Uva Ursi contains hydroquinnones including arbutin; flavonoids including quercitin; tannins, volatile oils and iridoids. It is indicated for painful urination, cystitis and any inflammatory conditions of the urinary tract. These statements have not been evaluated by the FDA.

You can find Uva Ursi in capsules, tinctures and as "bulk", loose herbs at health food stores.

VALERIAN ROOT, *Valeriana officinalis,* is an indispensable herb for dog and horse owners (and for our use) when calming of the nervous system is required. Valerian reduces anxiety. It is used for treatment of seizures and head pain/injuries. It is rich in magnesium and niacin which are nourishing to the nerves.

For horses, we feed the cut and sifted dry root, a tablespoon daily for calming. You can also cook the root into a syrup:

Place 1/2 cup dry root into 3 quarts of boiling, pure water (enameled/glass pot)

Simmer for 30 minutes, covered, then leave to steep for one hour

Strain the decoction and add 1 and 1/2 cups brown sugar

Return to the heat and cook the sugar into the liquid just barely at a simmer for 5 minutes

Preserve the mixture with 1 level teaspoon grapefruit seed extract mixed in well (carefully - this extract is strong and will blister your skin full strength)

Feed one ounce (30cc's) when needed for calming

Note: Valerian root is not allowed at equine competitions.

For dogs, the tincture or capsules are good choices.
Dose by weight - the recommended human adult dose for dogs over 125 lbs;
use 1/2 that dose for dogs from 50 to 125 lbs.;
1/4 that dose for dogs 30 to 50 lbs;
1/8 dose for smaller dogs.

Put alcohol tincture into a little hot water to evaporate the alcohol before dosing the cooled liquid.

Humans can drink the decoction, take the tincture or capsules to treat epilepsy, stress, ulcers, coughs and bronchitis, migraines, heart palpitation, spasms, addictions to drugs or alcohol and to get a good night's sleep.

Valerian has a vermifuge effect - it helps to expel parasites/worms.

VITEX, *chaste tree berries,* are used for horses with blood sugar imbalances; for women during menopause; for aggressiveness and to regulate the glands. We feed them whole by the small handful daily to horses in their bucket feeds.

WHITE WILLOW BARK, *Salix alba,* is "Nature's Aspirin". I remember a product from my youth called "willoprin" - tablets made of powdered white willow bark and slippery elm. I carried the little metal box with me always and took the tablets when others would have taken aspirin.

The bark contains Salicin and Tannin. White Willow is actually used to *heal digestive tract debilities*, so it is not an ulcer inducing compound like regular aspirin is (which is synthesized from the medium of the bark). It can be used for pain and inflammation relief for people, horses and dogs but never for cats. Just as aspirin tablets can be deadly for the feline; white willow bark's salicin is contraindicated!

Horses can be fed the cut and sifted bark (1/4 cup per feeding) or powdered (2 tablespoons) mixed into the hard feed or mash. It will test at competitions, so be aware if you are a show rider. Many herbs are not allowed at equine competitions; they are considered a performance enhancer even though they are used as healing agents.

Dogs can be given the tablets - from 1/2 to 2 tabs every 12 hours depending upon weight.

People take the tablets at the same doses and rates as regular OTC aspirin tablets.

WOOD BETONY, *Betonica officinalis,* is an herb used to calm people while supporting the central nervous system. For horses, it was traditionally used for glandular disorders, to support the spleen and digestion and for arthritis. It was added to a bucket feed or mash using only the aerial parts - above ground.

Wood Betony is full of calcium with potassium and magnesium in smaller amounts. These minerals nourish the nerves, joints and the muscles of the digestive tract.

It can be brewed into a tea for the horse (I have used the tea myself to relax when under stress) that is poured over a bucket feed or offered alone in a bucket to drink. As with any unfamiliar herb, offer a small amount at first and watch for any adverse reaction. If this occurs, do not give any more of the herb, because all animals are unique and have varying metabolisms.

There are three ways of addressing dis-ease:

The Scientific Tradition uses chemistry to alleviate symptoms.

The Heroic Tradition uses herbs in a similar way to address the disorder according to the herbal effects.

The Wisdom Way nourishes the body to support its own innate healing.

There is a place for each of these Traditions in healing.

We maintain an herbal stable yard - basing our equine rations and care upon the simplicity of Nature and our belief that good health is the natural condition and we nourish it with all we do. Bodies know how to heal. We work hard to support the systems that make healing possible.

YARROW, *Achillea millefolium,* reputedly used to treat wounds during the Trogan wars, its Latin name is derived from the Greek hero, Achilles. I have used it as an infusion to drench (dose horses orally) my horses when the barn where they boarded was overcome by a severe respiratory tract infection. My geldings were the only horses not on antibiotics and they recovered first. A strong tea brewed from the flowers was used many times per day and I actually bathed their bodies with the "tea" and covered them with anti-sweat coolers to break their fevers. On this occasion, I added colloidal silver to their drenches, as well.

Yarrow tea is a profound healer of colds and flu in humans (boneset herb is added for flu to reduce aches and pain). Yarrow steam from a pot of boiled water can be inhaled to break up mucus. Yarrow blossom infusions are used orally after giving birth to slow the bleeding. It is styptic in its actions externally as well. DURING PREGNANCY, Yarrow is contraindicated.

Yarrow infusion can be used as an ear lotion for dogs. If your dog has external allergies, avoid Yarrow as it might cause a reaction.

Yarrow flower essence is used to alleviate a sense of vulnerability; for shyness.

The Following Herbs Should Not Be Used During Pregnancy/Gestation or Lactation.*
*without consultation with a health care practitioner

BALMONY
BARBERRY
BLACK COHOSH
BLADDERWRACK
BLACK WALNUT (this one *never* for any horses!)
BLUE VERVAIN
BLESSED THISTLE
BONESET
BORAGE
BUCHU
BUCK BEAN
CATNIP
CHAMMOMILE
COLTSFOOT
COMFREY
CUCKOO FLOWER
DAMIANA
DONG QUAI
EPHEDRA

FEVER FEW
GOLDENSEAL
GUARANA
HERB ROBERT
HOREHOUND
HORSE CHESTNUT
HYSSOP
LICORICE
LOBELIA
MOTHERWORT
MUGWORT
MYRRH
OREGON GRAPE ROOT
OSHA ROOT!!
PENNY ROYAL
PRICKLY ASH
RED ROOT
RED CLOVER
RUE
SAFFLOWER
SHEPHERDS PURSE
STONECROP
TANSEY
TARRAGON
UVA URSI
VERVAIN
WILD YAM
WOOD SAGE
YARROW (is used after delivery to check bleeding)
YELLOW DOCK
This is, by no means, a complete list - but covers some of the common herbs that are potentially dangerous during pregnancy. Consult with an herbalist or practitioner about any herb you are considering for a pregnant being.

Methods
The different ways to prepare herbs are part of a tradition that extracts the healing properties according to the parts used, i.e.-blossoms, leaves, berries, bark or roots. The softer and more fragile the plant part, the less heat is used for extraction. The harder the part (bark, root, berry), the more heat is needed. Some herbs are only viable for extraction in alcohol or saliva, such as Osha root. And some herbs release their properties in tepid water, such as Senna pods.

Blossoms & Leaves are made into infusions by pouring pure water just off the boil onto the dry or fresh herbs and allowing the mixture to steep for 15 to 30 minutes before drinking. This infusion can be added to a horse's bran mash, mixed into a dog's dry food or strained for tea for a human.

Roots, Berries & Barks:These tougher parts of herbs are actually boiled into a decoction. The herb is placed into a pot of pure water, covered, brought to a boil and simmered for 15 to 30 minutes. Then the mixture is left covered to cool before use.

Oils & Ointments are made by infusing a vegetable oil (olive, walnut, sesame or safflower) with the herbs. You can use a double boiler to heat the oil with herbs added for an hour or so, simmering the water - not the oil, or place the herbs in oil in a bottle in a very warm place for 2 weeks. Use the oil after straining or create ointment by adding beeswax (one fourth part wax to three fourth parts oil) to the strained oil and slowly melting it before pouring into jars to set.

Always use non-metal pots and utensils when working with herbs. Metals will alter the volatile oils.

So many chemical insecticides and herbicides are used now throughout the world that we are seeing, as a result, much disease, many tumors in people and animals and even the death of pollinating bees that can eventually leave us without any food.

Fortunately, many of us are open to alternatives! Here are some available alternatives to buy:

Corn gluten based herbicides and fatty acid sprays

Yellow sticky traps for flying insects.

Boric Acid formulas, **Diatomaceous Earth** and **silica gel** for roaches

d-limonene spray for crawling insects

Neem oil for ant repellent (even in the kitchen; since Neem oil is safely used as toothpaste!)

Citronella candles and oil in sprays to repel mosquitoes (also **Gerinol** from geraniums)

Pyrethrin sprays (from chrysanthemums)

beneficial, predatory insects like lady bugs, mantises, fly predator wasps, etc.

BT Dunks in standing water to prevent mosquitoes

The *Journal of Pesticide Reform* reported that *Glyphosphate* (a well known herbicide) has caused testicular tumors in male and thyroid cancer in female rodents. Increases in kidney, pancreatic and liver tumors have also been seen in experimental studies. Home pesticide use resulted in a risk 4 times higher for childhood Leukemia; brain cancer is associated with use of pesticides to control termites, shampoos with lindane, flea collars and liquid on pets, diazinon and carbaryl in the garden. Permethrin (a synthetic Pyrethrin) has been believed to be carcinogenic after limited trials.

So, at Naturalpaths, we promote herbal alternatives! And here are a few recipes:

Dog flea/tick powder - equal parts Rosemary/Thyme/Sage powders (ground herbs)

Cat flea/tick powder - equal parts Sage/Lavender powdered herbs (rosemary and thyme have phenol which can be bad for cats!)

Insect repellent spray for Horses - to a one quart spray bottle add 20 drops essential oil of Citronella, 20 drops oil of Rosemary, 20 drops Eucalyptus oil, 40 drops Cedarwood oil, 20 drops Patchouli oil, 20 drops Clove oil and half cider vinegar, half water to fill. Shake often.

Insect repellent spray for people - to an 8 ounce bottle add 10 drops citronella oil, 5 drops cedarwood oil, 5 drops clove oil, 5 drops patchouli oil and 5 drops eucalyptus oil then fill with water and shake often.

A few years ago I was a vendor at a health fair and I was giving away one ounce containers of our dog and cat flea repellent powders from a big basket with the recipes on it. I got a phone call that night from a man asking me if he could use the dog flea powder on chicken. I said that I had never used it on chickens, but it was non-toxic, just organic herbs... he said "not chicken**s** - CHICKEN - to cook it, the stuff smells so good." I told him, after a moment to compose myself, that it certainly was safe to cook with.

That is a testimonial to safe, alternative methods to repel pests.

28469121R00023

Made in the USA
Middletown, DE
15 January 2016